Journal of The Wandering Mind

Tasmia Chowdhury

Journal of the wandering Mind; Pain, Love, Fantasy
© 2022 Tasmia Chowdhury

Presentation by *BookLeaf Publishing*

Web: www.bookleafpub.com

E-mail: info@bookleafpub.com

ISBN: 9789357445634

First edition 2022

Drown

There is so much inside my head that sometimes it feels
like I'm drowning,
Always gasping for breath,
But my body seems to fail me,
too much;
Yet-
Never enough,
This never-ending spiral,
Sinking in to my bones,
Destruction takes over,
A pretty blindfold,
Damage wraps around my skin

Happiness

Haunted,
Nightmares from the past,
Restless heart,
Everlasting grief,
Thirsting,
Hoping,
Begging,
Praying,
Wishing for just one chance,
But watching,
As every opportunity,
Drifts away,
The desire for happiness,
Simply too much to take

Truth

The truth is always hard to bare, but this is one that I must share.
For you see,
the truth is that I've always cared,
At times, too much,
And others-
Perhaps not quite enough,
The truth is,
I have never valued myself,
Easily giving in,
Letting people take advantage,
Eventually thinking; no even believing,
I deserved nothing-
Only pain, regret, punishment,
However,
I am learning,
Discovering,
That the truth is,
Far more complex than that,
The truth is,
I wear my heart on my sleeve,
And feel everything 10x's deep,
The truth is
I am more than harsh words,
And empty jokes,
And this life I lead,
Has infinite journeys to go

Desire

He was like a raging fire,
One I desperately sought to burn.
His gaze icy,
Irises filled with embers of molten black.
A trembling blizzard lingering beneath.
As his hands find their way,
Slowly wrapped around me,
Entangled,
As we sway beneath the gentle wind.
There is no wish to escape,
His lips descend upon mine.
A rose without thorns,
His touch too soft,
This poison too sweet,
His love was madness,
Pure and tender.
His voice,
The last straw to insanity,
For in that moment,
I knew,
Only death could be this divine

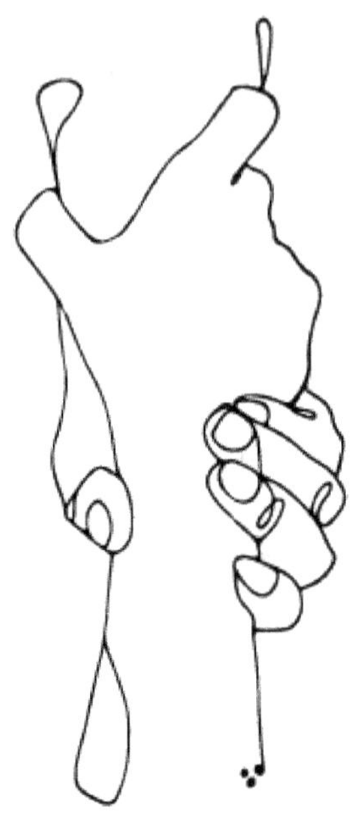

Red

Blanketed in darkness,
Watching,
As the blade caresses my skin,
My head starts spinning,
When I turn,
Constantly surrounded by crimson,
Hoping,
Pleading,
Crying,
Praying,
Knowing,
This wasn't the girl,
I was meant to be,
The one who pretended to smile and laugh,
While she was down and hurt,
Unable to sit and cry,
Slowly wondering when,
She began to seek comfort in her pain,
Not realizing,
She was beginning to kill herself

Siren Song

Eyes like the ocean,
Voice ever-present,
Unyielding waves,
Calm before any storm,
Drawing me in,
Only- to never pull me out,
I am falling; sinking,
Yet-
I feel as if I am floating,
His breath fills my lungs,
Encasing my soul,
Delirious,
I gasp,
Warmth,
Comfort,
Safety,
How is it possible,
That in these arms,
I have finally arrived home

Bleed

If I could
I would cut myself open
Watching as I bled
Slowly reaching within this chest
I'd rip this heart that beats
Oceans of red flowing
Till nothing else mattered
If it meant
I was gifted the opportunity
To set you free

Smile

Behind the smile lays regret
Ruined by emotions
Only wishing for someone to notice
To truly care
Until she understood her pain would never vanish
A futile wish
Disappointed expectations
She learned first-hand
Sometimes there really isn't someone
We can fully put our trust in

Hideaway

It has become a pain that lingers
As mountains of ignorance surround her
The desire to run and hide
From this never-ending game
that is life
Yet everywhere she turns
Past the deserts of sadness
She is unable to see

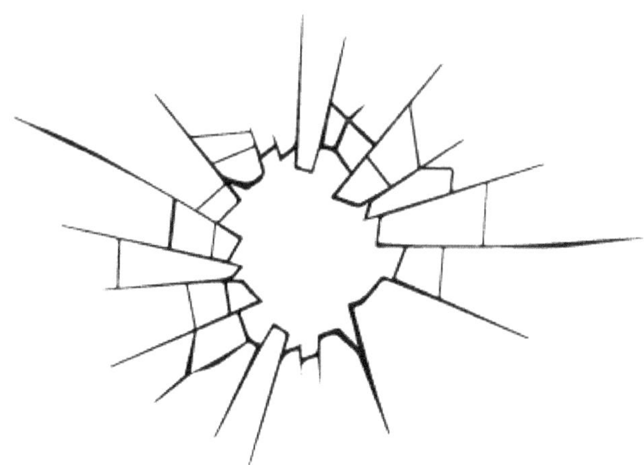

Letter to My Father

To My Father;
There are many things I wish to say
But for now I will settle for this
Thank you
Thank you for being the man that you are
For always loving me so deeply
Thank you
For always accepting me
And staying by my side
For being here when my days are light
And especially when they become endlessly dark
Thank you
For always holding my hand and hugging me tight
On the days I couldn't breathe and nothing seemed right
When my world began to crumble and shake
Thank you
For always giving me strength
And picking me up when I fall
Thank you
For giving me courage
Especially when it feels like
I have none at all
But most importantly
Thank you
Thank you
For simply and always loving me
Even when I don't believe I deserve it all

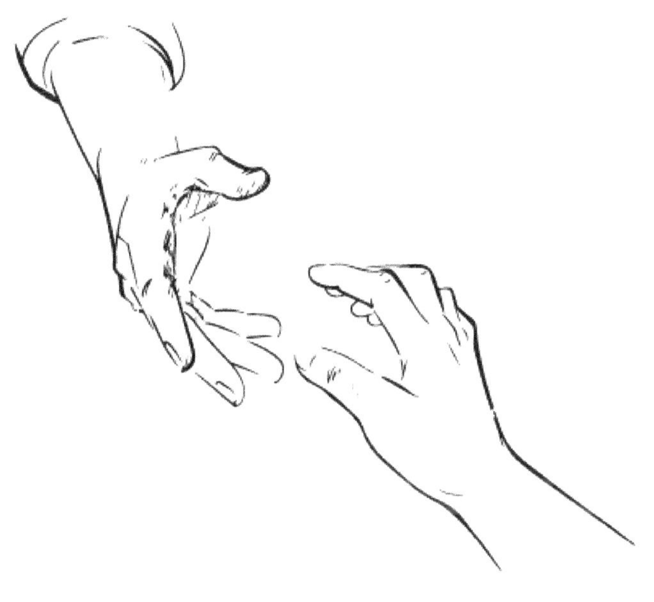

Choices

I feel like I'm doomed,
Failed to make the same repeated mistakes,
Masked or disguised as decisions or alternate choices,
Where only my reality is different,
But the situations and emotions,
Never change,
Maybe I have no happy ending or happily ever after,
But perhaps I hope,
I foolishly hope,
That maybe just maybe,
I haven't lived long enough to tell

Echoes of Loneliness Corner

The echoes of loneliness corner are the sounds I hear as my sister goes to sleep by me every night.
They are the laughs that quiet down when I slowly come in sight.
It is the thought that I make the atmosphere bitter.
The feeling of watching my parents and sister fill with joy and laughter, but my brain telling me, to them I am only a stranger.
It is physically sitting in a room where your body is present.
But your mind- your mind begs to wander.
It is when your muscles tense with the prayer to remain unseen, and escape questions for which you have no answer.
The reality is, the echoes of loneliness corner, are the darkest parts of my mind.
The ravenous hunger to be spread and uncovered.
They make me weak and scared but mostly tired.
Exhausted and fragile.
The belief that if I let them take over,
how can I possibly remain human?

The Desire To Be My Mother's Daughter

Mother,
Describing how much I love you
sometimes feels like the most difficult thing in the world
to do.
Sometimes I feel like I love you so much that my words
become numb as I can hardly breathe.
Others- I feel like perhaps I don't think I love you as
much as I could or maybe even should.
There are times when I hurt you,
words sharp like daggers.
Even when it's not your fault.
Yet there you are,
always accepting this anger and frustration.
Soothing it with gentle warmth, only someone like you
can muster.
Always accepting my apologies,
when I know you deserve better.
No matter how much we fight or argue,
it will always be your arms that I will forever turn too.
You have always been my light,
protecting me, when I am surrounded by darkness and
shadows.
Becoming my shield, when I am no longer able.
Your embrace,
my medication and healing.

Your prayers,
my blessings and feelings.
Your pain,
Your hurt,
Your tears,
My strength, for living
Breathing,
and dreaming.
Your heart,
a place I am grateful to be received in.
Oh my darling mother!
This heart,
This soul,
This mind,
This body,
I promise to become someone,
You will be proud to believe in.

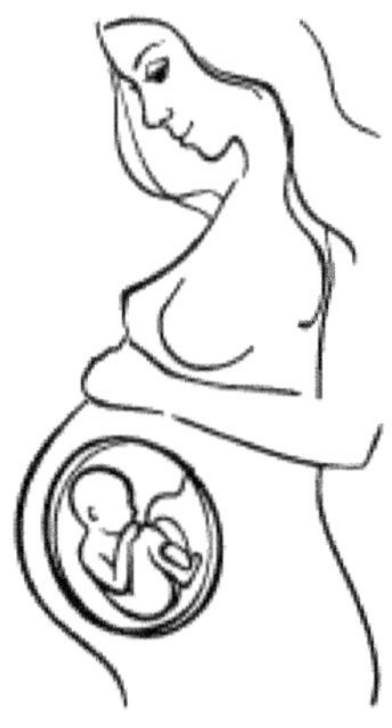

I Am

To the world,
I am rude,
I am lazy,
I don't think before I speak,
I judge to quickly,
Make decisions without really thinking,
I am naïve,
I am gullible,
I am sheltered,
I am too innocent,
However,
To myself,
I am a constant work in progress-
Forever evolving,
Changing,
Quietly shaping and molding,
A gentle, patient, sturdy yet stunning,
masterpiece in the making

Dream

I want to live in my dreams,
The place where suddenly all these voices in my head
remain quiet.
The desire so strong,
I can practically taste it.
This place where happiness and success have no
correlation.
And my worth and value,
Cannot be equated to a cheque I must deposit I want to
escape somewhere,
I can be blessed.
The freedom to spread my wings,
Wherever this restless heart of mine can feel inspired.

Refuge

Sometimes I just long to leave everything behind.
to run and hide,
only to never be found again.
From this mind,
This body,
This heart,
This soul,
But I fear,
I will never find,
The solace and refuge,
I am desperately aching for.

Destination; Lost but Found

I want to get lost in this universe,
Discover the world I've yet to see,
Create my own wonderous galaxy.
I want to lay in heaps of snow,
Gaze upon mountains even though my nose is runny and
it's cold.
I want to laugh at night,
As I lay underneath a bed of stars,
I long to watch the sunrise,
Only to be left in awe as it begins to set,
I wish to get lost in a field of flowers,
And clear blue ocean waters,
But most importantly,
I want to finally allow myself,
The opportunity to live life,
Like I never have before

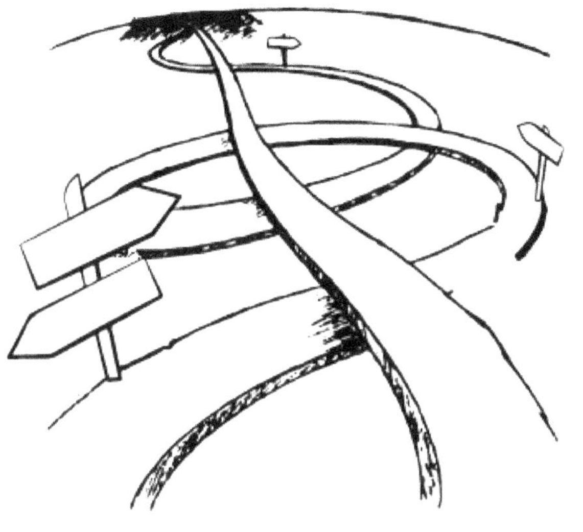

Inevitable

One day it will all make sense,
The pain,
The tears,
The heartache,
The anger,
The frustration,
The unavoidable mess that is known as life,
Even if my eyes are struggling to it through,
In the end,
I know,
Every struggle,
Every disappointment,
Every battle,
Every choice,
I have made up until this very moment,
Will have all been worth it

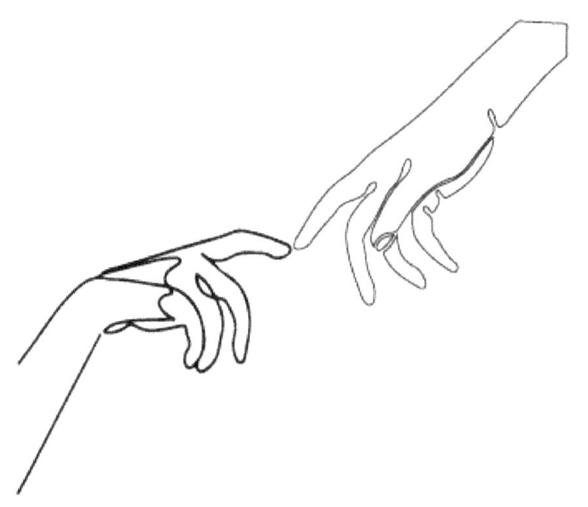

Love Me Tender

I am but a fragment of tender broken pieces,
Slowly being stitched back together,
By the love I have refused,
For so long,
Shining in the glow,
Of stars embraced by moonlight,
Hugged by the shadows,
As we dance together,
Illuminated,
There is no longer anything left to fight

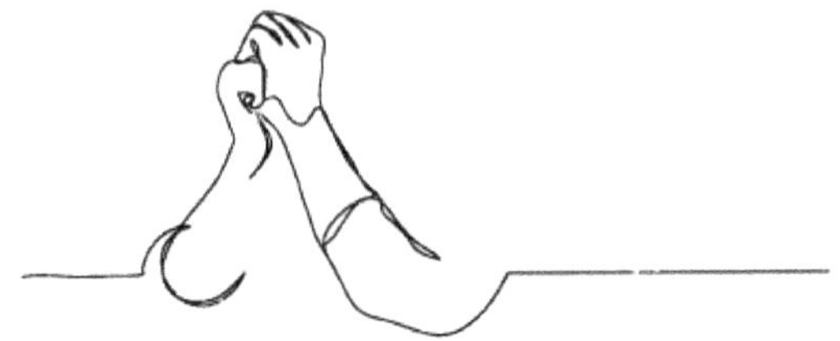

Beautiful Darkness

There is beauty in your darkness,
Sunshine in your tears,
Heaven in your hallowed heart,
Happiness among your fears,
All the broken, crumbled pieces of you,
Complete and utter,
Breathtaking,
Unspoken,
Perfection

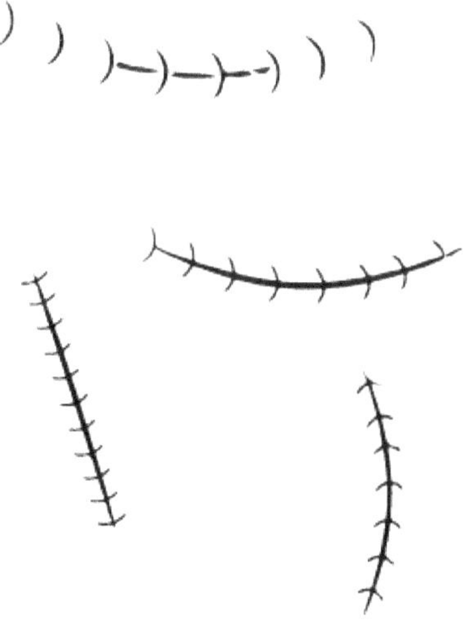

You

It is in your arms,
I find home.
Your eyes,
I seek hope.
Your voice,
I gather courage,
Your scent,
I am granted refuge.
As your soul,
Begins to collide with mine,
It is precisely in that moment,
I sense,
I truly belong